FRIENDSHIP

by Sharon Lee Roberts
illustrated by Linda Hohag

THE CHILD'S WORLD

Mankato, MN 56001

I wished for a friend,
an everyday friend,
a jumprope, somersault,
sliding-board friend,
a see-saw, roller-skate,
hopscotch friend,
who would stay and play
all day.

When I moved
next door to you,
my wishes all came true.

—Jane Belk Moncure
from *Wishes, Whispers, and Secrets*

Library of Congress Cataloging in Publication Data

Roberts, Sharon Lee, 1949-
  Friendship.

  (What is it?)
  Summary: Children demonstrate the meaning of
friendship through such gestures as keeping secrets,
sharing disappointments, and making little sacrifices.
  1. Friendship—Juvenile literature.   [1. Friendship]
I. Hohag, Linda, ill.   II. Title.   III. Series.
BF575.F66R62   1986   302.3'4   86-9641
ISBN 0-89565-350-8

It's nice to have a friend. It's nice
to be a friend. What is friendship?

Friendship is sharing your last stick
of bubble gum, even though—with half
a stick—you won't be able to blow as
big a bubble.

Friendship is holding a friend up
while she learns to roller-skate.

Friendship is sharing your books and
your toys.

And when you've been playing at a friend's house, friendship is helping pick up.

When you are playing with one friend
and another friend stops by,

friendship is doing something all of
you can do together.

When you're in a hurry to go out to play, friendship is waiting for a friend to put on his boots.

Friendship is sharing good times and
laughing together over silly things,

like the time you put the ruffled
bonnet on Charger, your big sable
and white collie.

When a friend has slipped and fallen in a mud puddle — and everyone is laughing — friendship is helping him up.

When you're feeling sad because you were not invited to a party, you can tell a friend and know he will understand.

And friendship is listening to his secrets
without telling them to anyone
else.

When a friend has been in an accident and can't come out to play, friendship is taking a book to him.

Friendship is helping a friend
collect rocks, because you know
it's his favorite thing to do.

When your ice cream slips off the cone, a friend will feel sad with you.

When a friend sleeps over, friendship is letting her have the top bunk even though you love it up there.

Friendship means you think about a
friend. . .

even though you might be apart.

Friendship can be shared with all kinds of people—family, teachers, neighbors. A friend can be any age.